KT-484-360

This book belongs to:

_____

_____

Exploring

ALAIN GRÉE
Exploring

Button
BOOKS

AIRPORT

152
BUS

FOREST

Park

GO

Shops

First published 2013 by Button Books, an imprint of Guild of Master Craftsman Publications Ltd, Castle Place, 166 High Street, Lewes, East Sussex BN7 1XU.

Text © GMC Publications Ltd, 2013 Copyright in the Work © GMC Publications Ltd, 2013 Illustrations © 2013 A.G. & RicoBel.

ISBN 978 1 90898 511 8

All rights reserved. The right of Alain Grée to be identified as the author of this work has been asserted in accordance with the Copyright, Designs and Patents Act 1988, sections 77 and 78.

No part of this publication may be reproduced, stored in a retrieval system or transmitted in any form or by any means without the prior permission of the publisher and copyright owner.

Whilst every effort has been made to obtain permission from the copyright holders for all material used in this book, the publishers will be pleased to hear from anyone who has not been appropriately acknowledged and to make the correction in future reprints.

The publishers and author can accept no legal responsibility for any consequences arising from the application of information, advice or instructions given in this publication.

A catalogue record for this book is available from the British Library.

Publisher: Jonathan Bailey; Production Manager: Jim Bulley; Managing Editor: Gerrie Purcell; Senior Project Editors: Sara Harper and Cath Senker; Managing Art Editor: Gilda Pacitti; Art Editor: Rebecca Mothersole; Colour origination by GMC Reprographics; Printed and bound in China.

At home

This is a big house. What can you see in each room?
Which room is missing from this house?

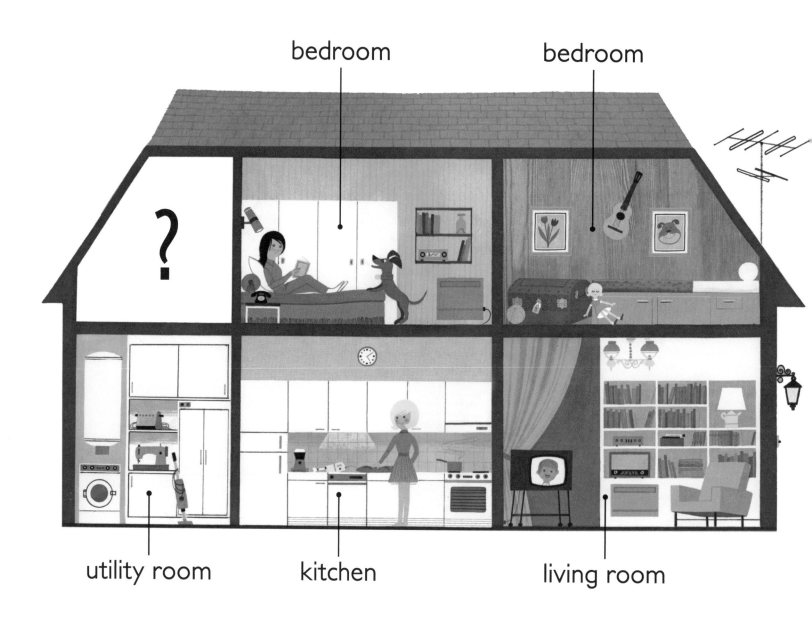

bedroom

bedroom

?

utility room

kitchen

living room

What is your home like?

What can you see from your room?

Let's go and have
a look outside.

In the garden

Some houses
have a garden.

Birds and
animals
sometimes
come into
gardens.

Which animals can
you see in this garden?
Are there any flowers?
What colours are they?

Look up!
What can you see?

In the town

Shops

On the high street there are shops. What does this shop sell?

Look – a toy shop!
Which toy would you choose?

What can you buy here?

Places to visit

Do you have any of these
places near your home?
Which have you visited?
What did you see there?

Match the words with the pictures.

zoo
museum
railway station
funfair

Exploring the park

What are all the people doing in the park?

How many games can you spot being played?

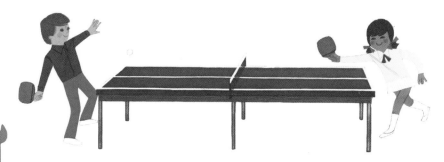

15

In the countryside

In the countryside, there are trees, fields and flowers.

This girl is going to pick some wild flowers in a field.

Exploring a farm

Farms are in the countryside. Farmers grow tasty fruit for us to eat.

Can you name the different kinds of fruit?

What else do farmers grow?

Many farms have animals.

Here are some farm animals.

cow

sheep

goat

pig

chickens

Which animals can you find in the barn?

Exploring the woods

The woods have many trees. It is cool, dark and shady.
Shhh! If you are very quiet, you might spot some animals.
Some live on the ground and others live in the trees.
Which animals can you see? Can you count them?

Exploring rivers and streams

You can spot many animals near rivers and streams. These animals can swim in the water, cling on to rocks or fly around.

Frogs and ducks
live near water.

Some people like to
go fishing in rivers.

fox

owl

fish

frog

pig

Do these animals live in the woods, on a farm or in a river?

squirrel

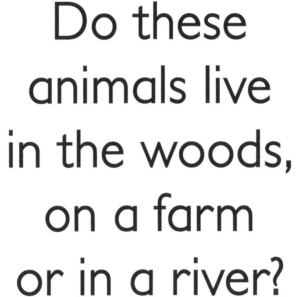

goat

cow

duck

woods

farm

river

Travelling to new places

How can you explore your local area?
You can travel in different ways.
Which is your favourite way to get around?

bus

bike

taxi

walking

boat

car

scooter

29

Exploring other countries

The world is a big place! You can travel a
long way away to explore other countries.

Have you ever visited another country? Did you get there by aeroplane, train or boat?

aeroplane

train

boat

Countries around the world

Do you know anyone who lives in another country?
Have you ever visited them?

Children in other countries may eat different foods.

They may speak another language. Perhaps they play different games.

Exploring hot places

Some plants and animals are found
only in countries where it is very hot.

parrot

tropical fruits

toucan

lizard

kangaroo

camel

This is a desert. Deserts are the
hottest places in the world and only
a few animals and plants can live there.

Exploring cold places

In very cold countries, it often snows.
Snow is fun. You can ski on snowy
slopes. Or why not build a snowman?

Try sliding downhill
on a sledge in the snow.

Ice skating is great fun, too.

You will need
somewhere cosy to
warm up afterwards!

Exploring high places

Mountains are very high places. To explore them, people use special equipment. Here are some of the things they need. Can you find them in the picture?

helmet
gloves
ice axe
boots
ropes
goggles

Exploring further

We know little about many parts of our world. Few people have visited the freezing cold Antarctic or the deep, dark oceans. Parts of the rainforests are unexplored, too. Which places would you like to explore?

Exploring at night

One evening, before you go to bed, why not look out of your window? What can you see?

Can you see the Moon
and stars in the night sky?
Try using a star map to find
out the names of the stars.

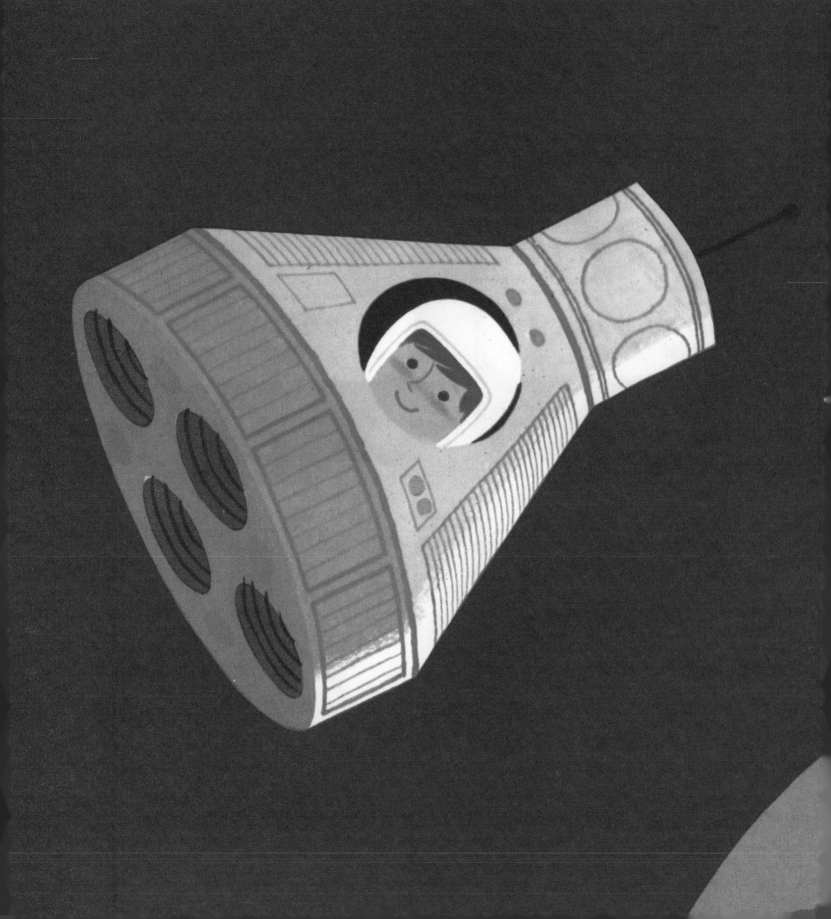

Exploring space

Astronauts go into space to explore. A rocket launches their spacecraft. The spacecraft can land on the Moon.

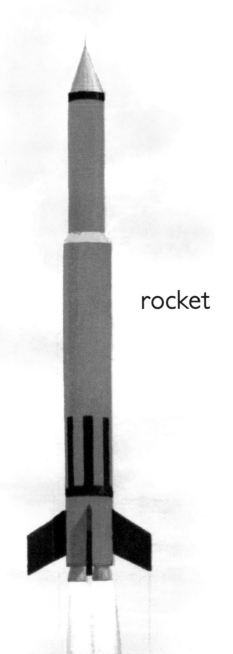

rocket

To explore the Moon, astronauts wear special spacesuits.

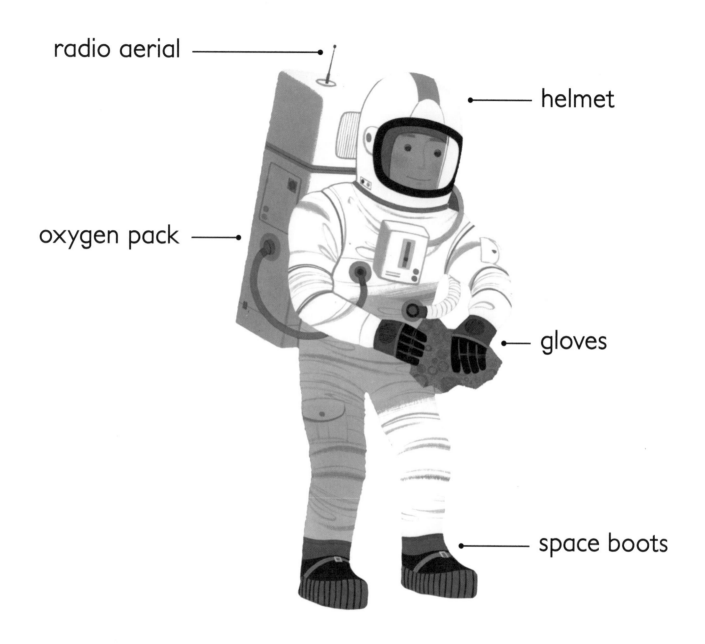

radio aerial

helmet

oxygen pack

gloves

space boots

From the Moon, astronauts can see planet Earth.
Maybe one day we will be able to explore other
planets in space.

For more on Button Books, contact:

GMC Publications Ltd
Castle Place, 166 High Street, Lewes, East Sussex, BN7 1XU
United Kingdom
Tel +44 (0)1273 488005
www.buttonbooks.com